FIRST AMERICANS

The Seminole

DAVID C. KING

Marshall Cavendish
Benchmark
New York

ACKNOWLEDGMENTS

Series consultant: Raymond Bial

Marshall Cavendish Benchmark
99 White Plains Road
Tarrytown, New York 10591-9001
www.marshallcavendish.us

Text copyright © 2007 by Marshall Cavendish Corp.
Map and illustrations copyright © 2007 by Marshall Cavendish Corp.
Map and illustrations by Christopher Santoro

Library of Congress Cataloging-in-Publication Data
King, David C.
The Seminole / by David C. King.
p. cm. — (First Americans)
Includes bibliographical references and index.
ISBN-13: 978-0-7614-2253-2
ISBN-10: 0-7614-2253-6
1. Seminole Indians—History—Juvenile literature. 2. Seminole
Indians—Social life and customs—Juvenile literature. I. Title. II.
Series: First Americans (Benchmark Books (Firm)
E99.S28K56 2006
975.9004'973—dc22
2006011977

Photo research by Joan Meisel
Cover Photo: Lake County Museum/Corbis
The photographs in this book are used by permission and through the courtesy of: Alamy: 28, North Wind Picture Archives;
33, Ace Stock Limited; Corbis: 4, Franz Marc Frei; 8, 30, Bettmann; 12, David Muench; 21, Lake County Museum;
Getty Images: 9, 10, Hulton Archive; North Wind Picture Archives: 7, 16, 23, 36, 40, 41; Courtesy, National Museum of the American Indian,
Smithsonian Institution: 18 (L00332); Peter Arnold, Inc.: 1, Michael J. Minardi; 39, Peter Frischmuth; Raymond Bial: 14, 24.

Editor: Tara T. Koellhoffer
Editorial Director: Michelle Bisson
Art Director: Anahid Hamparian
Series designer: Symon Chow

Printed in China
1 3 5 6 4 2

CONTENTS

1 · THE PEOPLE AND THE LAND

If you could have visited Florida in the year 1800, you would have seen a beautiful land that was home to several thousand Native Americans. Most of these people were Seminole Indians. They lived on fertile land in northern Florida. They had prosperous farms and sturdy log houses. By 1860, the Seminole had moved to the huge wetlands in southern Florida called the Everglades. They shared this land of swamps and grasses with snakes and alligators and swarms of mosquitoes.

The "Runaways"

In the 1700s, the thirteen colonies on the Atlantic coast of North America were growing rapidly. In 1775, the colonies began to fight to win their independence from England. As American settlements expanded, the pioneers took over Indian lands.

The Everglades are one of the largest wetland areas in the world.

The Creek Indians were one of the tribes squeezed out by American settlers. Some of the tribal leaders launched a series of wars to try to save their lands and their way of life. Throughout the 1700s, more and more Creek bands headed south from the Carolinas and Georgia into Florida. By the time of the American Revolution, several thousand Indians had joined this migration. They were called Seminole from the Spanish word *cimarron*, meaning "wild."

Throughout the 1700s and early 1800s, the Seminole were hardworking and prosperous farmers and traders. A few hundred African Americans who had escaped slavery lived with them. The Seminole accepted these newcomers. In addition to growing crops, the Seminole hunted and fished. They traded dried fish, deerskins, beeswax, and honey to the Spanish who held Florida as a colony.

A Troubled History

Around 1800, American settlers began to push into Florida. The American government supported plantation owners who went to

21

Men prepared the soil and women planted the crops.

The Seminole feared General Andrew Jackson.

Florida to find escaped slaves. In 1817, the government sent General Andrew Jackson into Florida with a force of soldiers and volunteers. Jackson was ruthless in fighting what was later called the First Seminole War. His men burned villages, destroyed crops, and seized Spanish towns. The rulers of Spain realized they could not defeat the Americans. In 1819, Spain ceded Florida to the United States.

To avoid more bloodshed, in 1823, several Seminole chiefs agreed to move onto a 4-million-acre (1.6-million-hectare) reservation in the middle of

Florida. For the next few years, the Seminole struggled to restore their way of life in this new, more difficult environment.

The Seminole people faced more hardship in the next decade. Andrew Jackson became president of the United States. In 1830, he signed the Indian Removal Act. All eastern tribes had to move west, beyond the Mississippi River, to land called Indian Territory (now the state of Oklahoma). Throughout the 1830s, tribe after tribe was forced to move to Indian Territory.

In the Second Seminole War, Seminole leader Osceola's warriors attacked an army blockhouse.

Osceola: The Seminole Hero

Although Osceola was not a chief when the Second Seminole War began in 1835, older warriors and chiefs looked up to him. He planned his war against the U.S. Army carefully, always avoiding places where his men might be trapped. President Andrew Jackson, frustrated by Osceola's success, put nine different generals in command of the Florida troops. General Thomas Jessup finally tricked Osceola into coming to peace talks. Soldiers seized Osceola and took him to Fort Moultrie in Charleston, South Carolina. He died there a few months later; some said he died of a broken heart.

Osceola continued to inspire the Seminole long after his capture and death.

In Florida, the Seminole refused to move. They found a courageous young leader named Osceola, who organized their resistance in the Second Seminole War (1835–1842). Osceola used hit-and-run tactics to strike at the American troops, then disappear into the Everglades. For the United States, this conflict was the costliest of all the wars fought against the Native Americans. The government spent an estimated $40 million and lost around 1,500 soldiers.

After two years of fierce warfare, Osceola agreed to go to peace talks. It was a trick. U.S. soldiers seized Osceola, who was sick, and he died in a fort prison a few months later. The war dragged on until 1842, when almost 4,000 Seminole agreed to move to Indian Territory.

The Third Seminole War broke out in 1855. This time the Seminole were led by Chief Billy Bowlegs. This conflict was much less violent. It ended in 1858 when Billy Bowlegs agreed to lead more than 100 Seminole to Indian Territory. After 1858, the U.S. government gave up trying to force the rest of the Seminole to move to Indian Territory. These Seminole stayed in the Everglades, where their descendants still live today.

The Everglades

The Everglades are a beautiful region of grasslands, marsh, swamp, and open water. The Seminole call it Pa-May-Okee, which means "grassy water." The Everglades cover about 4,000 square miles (10,360 square km) in southern Florida. Much of the area is covered with **saw grass**, which can grow up to 15 feet (4.6 m). There are also many

The Seminole called the Everglades Pa-May-Okee, which means "grassy water," because of all the saw grass in the area.

small islands, called hammocks, that are usually covered with shrubs and trees.

The climate is mild with average monthly temperatures between 63 degrees F (17 degrees C) and 82 degrees F (28 degrees C). These conditions create an ideal environment for birds, especially waders, such as herons, egrets, and spoonbills. The Everglades are also home to alligators, snakes, and turtles, as well as deer, bears, and panthers. The Everglades were a harsh environment for humans. But for the Seminole, it became their homeland.

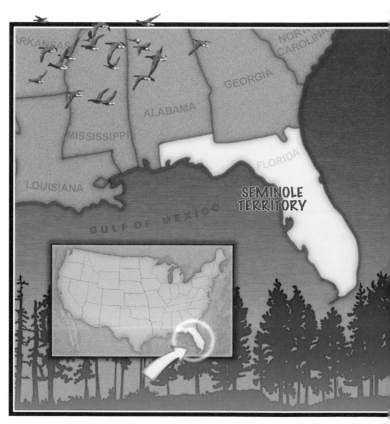

The Seminole originally lived in the fertile lands of northern Florida. Wars and settlers forced them to move south to the Everglades.

2 · THE SEMINOLE WAY OF LIFE

Throughout the 1850s, the Seminole people faced many changes. Now that they were in the marshy Everglades, they had to find new ways to live.

New Kinds of Homes

The Seminole began to build new kinds of homes. The men sank sturdy poles deep into the ground, then built a platform about 3 feet (1 m) off the ground. The women cut leaves from cabbage palms to make a roof.

The Seminole lived on a platform above the ground. There were no walls, so there were nice breezes all the time. They'd tie their belongings in bundles and hang them from the roof beams.

These houses, called **chickees**, were built on high ground. The scattered chickees were surrounded by open water, hidden from the lands outside the Everglades by acres of swamp and thick groves of cypress trees.

A chickee provided both shelter and cooling breezes.

Instead of walking on paths and roads, the Seminole now used the waterways of the Everglades. They made dugout canoes from a single cypress log. They burned away much of the log, then carved out the charred wood with tools.

Hunting, Fishing, and Gathering

There was not enough dry land to farm, but the Seminole were a resourceful people and made the most of what the Everglades provided. On the hammocks, they managed to grow corn, sweet potatoes, pumpkins, beans, squash, and

While one Seminole poles the canoe, another is ready for the hunt.

some sugarcane. They grew sunflowers for their seeds and oil. The Seminole also learned how to use many wild plants, including plums, berries, nuts, acorns, wild potatoes, and honey.

While the women tended the crops and gathered wild foods, the men fished and hunted. There were many kinds of fish and the Seminole had several ways to catch them. They used traps and nets, as well as hooks on a line, spears, and bows and arrows. Sometimes they used a poison that stunned the fish so the men could lift them out with nets.

The Seminole also hunted deer, rabbits, raccoons, wild turkeys, and birds like ducks and geese. They used deerskins for clothing and the bones of several animals to make tools and utensils. Wild hogs were a special treat since they provided tasty meat.

Mealtime

Seminole women prepared meals in the village cookhouse. The house was like all the other chickees, except that there was no raised platform, so the women had to build the fires on the ground.

The fire was made with five or six large logs laid flat in a circle, like the spokes of a wheel. The fire itself was started where the logs met. As they burned, the logs were pushed closer to the center. The women could sit on the unused parts of the logs while they prepared their meals.

The women made a pot of cornmeal mush called **sofkee**. The

A Seminole woman prepares a pot of sofkee (cornmeal mush) in the cookhouse.

Seminole Hot Cakes

This unusual dish makes a great breakfast. It can be a challenge if you're camping, but the Indians did it, often using a flat stone as a griddle. Notice that you'll be making two separate batches of batter.

You will need:

- 1³/4 cups cornmeal
- 1/2 teaspoon salt
- 1¹/2 teaspoons sugar
- 2 tablespoons cooking oil
- 3/4 cup boiling water
- 3/4 cup cold tap water
- 2 mixing bowls
- pancake griddle
- tea kettle
- maple syrup or jam
- clean towel
- serving plate
- adult helper

Makes 3–4 servings

1. With an adult's help, heat at least 1 cup of water to a boil in a tea kettle.
2. While the water heats, mix 3/4 cup cornmeal, salt, sugar, and 1 tablespoon cooking oil in a mixing bowl. Stir in 3/4 cup boiling water and mix only until blended.
3. In the other bowl, mix 1 cup cornmeal, 1 tablespoon cooking oil, and 3/4 cup cold water. Stir until blended.
4. Have your adult helper heat the griddle over medium heat. When it's hot enough that a drop of water bounces, grease the griddle with a little oil.
5. With the adult's help, pour enough of the hot-water batter to make a small pancake. Immediately pour the same amount of cold-water batter on top of the hot-water batter. You should be able to get two more pancakes on the griddle. Brown the hot cakes, flip them over, and brown the other side.
6. Place the hot cakes on a serving plate, cover them with a towel, and continue until you've used all the batter.
7. Serve with maple syrup or jam.

pot was kept warm all day, and people dipped into it whenever they were hungry. The Seminole also put fish, meat, potatoes, corn, squash, and beans into another large kettle to make a stew for their main meal. On some days, the people put pieces of meat or fish on sharpened sticks and roasted them over the fire.

Seminole Patchwork

When the Seminole moved to the hot, humid Everglades, they found that their heavy buckskin was not comfortable. They had to make dramatic changes in their clothing.

The Seminole exchanged their buckskin for clothing made of cotton cloth obtained from Spanish traders. They still needed clothing that covered them entirely because of mosquitoes and other insects. Women wore a long dress or skirt, with blouses like capes. Men wore leggings that covered the legs completely below the **breechcloth**. This was topped by a long, smock-like shirt belted at the waist. Children wore clothing much like that of their parents.

The Seminole loved decoration, and they developed distinctive styles that are still popular today. Many American Indian tribes used face and body paints for decoration. Since the Seminole were trying to keep themselves covered, they used clothing itself for decoration. They sewed strips of brightly colored cloth onto their garments, creating unique splashes of color. Men wore bandannas around their necks and turbans with large feathers attached on their heads.

Another change in Seminole clothing was the development of a decorative technique that became known as **Seminole patchwork**. Women cut out cloth into narrow strips, then sewed different-colored strips together to form an intricate

Both children and adults are fond of the colorful Seminole designs.

A Cautious Trade

When the Seminole were not at war with the Spanish, they carried on a cautious trade with the Spanish settlements and forts. They traded deerskins and dried fish for cloth and things made of iron, such as kettles, knives, and muskets.

Even after the Seminole wars against the U.S. Army, the Seminole approached American trading posts, hoping to trade for iron and cloth. The Americans were most impressed with the feathers the Seminole used for decoration, and a new, highly profitable trade developed. Americans in northern cities were eager for the feathers of the beautiful birds that lived in the Everglades, including swans, cranes, egrets, herons, and flamingos. Overhunting led to a sharp decline in the bird populations, however, and the U.S. government passed laws in the 1920s to protect the "plume birds."

Wading birds such as this heron were once hunted for their feathers. The birds of the Everglades are now protected.

patchwork design. At first Seminole women were trying to imitate the colorful stripes in Spanish clothing. But the women soon discovered that there was almost no limit to the number and variety of designs they could create. When the Seminole acquired sewing machines in the late 1800s, they could make patchwork shirts, dresses, and skirts much faster. Seminole patchwork remains popular today.

Seminole patchwork remains popular around the country today.

Changing Government

In the 1700s, the Seminole in Florida had a government in which each village or town was almost self-governing, or autonomous. The community had a "peace chief" and a "war chief." There was no one chief who ruled all of the towns. Instead, there was a tribal council made up of the oldest and wisest men. They helped the peace chiefs manage village affairs and make sure that food and other supplies would be stored so they would be available to families who needed them.

In times of war, the elders usually picked a younger man to lead, one with a reputation for skill in fighting. This was how Osceola was chosen to lead in the Second Seminole War, even though he was not a chief.

When the Seminole moved into the Everglades, their villages became even more independent. Villagers often had to make quick decisions, such as whether to fight or flee if they were attacked. In the 1840s and 1850s, when some chiefs agreed to sell their land or move to Indian Territory, others refused and kept their independence.

Seminole Patchwork

Seminole patchwork is fun, but it can also be complicated. For this project, you'll work with construction paper and glue instead of cloth and a sewing machine. You can use your completed patchwork as a notebook cover, a bookmark, or a greeting card. The directions here are for a band about 3 inches wide and 6 inches long. You can adjust the dimensions to make it larger or smaller.

You will need:
· pencil
· ruler
· 3 sheets of construction
   paper (any 3 colors you like)
· scissors
· white glue
· 2 sheets of white paper
· 1 sheet of black construction
   paper, or any dark color (optional)

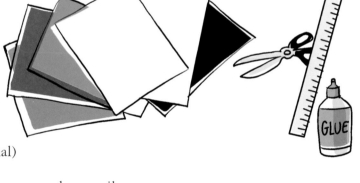

1· On 2 sheets of construction paper, use the pencil and ruler to measure a strip $6^1/4$ inches long and $1^1/4$ inches wide. Cut out the 2 strips.
2· On the third sheet of construction paper, measure and cut out a narrower strip, measuring $6^1/4$ inches by 1 inch.
3· Glue the 3 strips to a sheet of white paper, with the narrower strip in the middle.

Glue down with 1" strip in the middle

GLUE

4· Draw 4 lines across the strips 1¹/4 inches apart. Cut along those lines with scissors so that you have 5 smaller strips, each containing the 3 colors.

Draw 4 lines 1¹/4" apart

5· Place the strips on the second sheet of white paper. This time, tip them at an angle. The top and bottom of the middle strip should line up all the way across. When you're satisfied with how the strips look, glue them to the paper.

6· With the ruler and pencil, draw lines around your design. Plan the pencil lines so you'll lose as little of the design as possible.

7· Cut out the complete design; it should measure about 2 inches wide and 6¹/4 inches long.

Glue strips down at an angle

GLUE

8· Place your Seminole patchwork on a spiral notebook or on greeting card paper. If you like, you can make border strips about 1/2 inch wide out of black construction paper and glue these at the top and bottom of the design.

3 · CUSTOMS AND BELIEFS

When the Seminole moved into the Everglades in the mid-1800s, the villages became more widely scattered, separated by swamps and open water. The physical separation made each settlement more independent and self-reliant, with little sense of a government for the entire tribe.

Villages were made up of members of the same **clan**, and clan members were usually blood relatives. Each clan had a name such as Wolf, Heron, Panther, or West Wind. People always married people from different clans. Families often arranged marriages, but a woman could also try to attract a man by wearing ornaments.

Children belonged to their mother's clan, and the mother was most responsible for their early training. At birth, a small bag of herbs was tied around the baby's neck to ward off evil spirits. For the first two years, the infant spent most

Seminole villages were small and widely scattered.

of the day in a hammock, which the mother rocked while she worked.

Throughout childhood, boys and girls were taught to cooperate and help one another. There was no sense of competition or striving to be the best. Girls learned to take care of crops; harvest wild foods; make clothing, baskets, and other items; and prepare meals. Boys were taught to hunt and fish and to make tools and weapons.

The Green Corn Ceremony

The one event that most unified the Seminole tribe was the annual Green Corn Ceremony. This ancient tradition dates back to the days when the ancestors of today's Seminole were part of the Creek people. It is still held for four to eight days when the corn ripens in August.

The festival was an important time of renewal and coming together. Crimes committed against the village, or against an individual person, were judged by a council of elders. Debts were paid and old disputes were settled. Couples also married at the festival. In addition, boys who had turned thirteen or fourteen officially became adults and were given new names to show their adult status.

Until the late 1900s, medicine men played an important part in the Green Corn Festival. The medicine man took the **"medicine bundle"** from where he kept it hidden and prayed that he

Mothers kept their children with them all day while they worked. They often rocked their babies in hammocks.

The Seminole in Oklahoma

During the Seminole wars of the mid-1800s, most of the Seminole were forced to move to Indian Territory. Throughout the 1800s, each tribe received a parcel of land and established a government modeled after that of the United States. At first, the Seminole were placed in the western part of the Creek lands, but after considerable protest, they were given their own area. Various land reforms around 1900 granted some land to individual Indians, while other lands were opened to homesteaders and former slaves. In 1906, tribal governments were officially dissolved, but some areas continued to operate as informal reservations.

The Seminole population of Oklahoma today is estimated at 6,000 people or more. For much of the twentieth century, the Oklahoma Seminole abandoned many of their traditional customs and ways of living. In recent years, however, the people of many Indian tribes have started to take new pride in the traditions of their tribes. Many Seminole are working hard to preserve tribal ways, both in Florida and in Oklahoma.

The Seminole today practice many of their traditional crafts, such as basket making.

was worthy to take care of its sacred objects. The bundle contained many items, such as bits of horn, feathers, stones, and herbs that were symbols of everything the tribe needed for its survival and well-being.

The festival was not all solemn. Much of it was devoted to feasting, dancing, and games. A favorite game was like a combination of stickball and lacrosse. The women played against the men. Each team tried to hit a small tree with a ball that was about the size of a golf ball. Men used only a long wooden scoop, but women were allowed to use their hands.

Religious Beliefs

Like most Native American societies, the Seminole believed that everything in the world had a soul or spirit. This meant they were surrounded by plants and animals and objects with which they had to live in harmony. There were many kinds of prayers to keep spirits friendly. Hunters, for example, had to be careful not to offend the spirits of whatever animal they killed. This turned hunting into a religious act, with certain rituals and taboos. The Seminole believed that each animal species had a special "chief" that would seek revenge against any hunter who was cruel. These beliefs helped the Seminole maintain a delicate balance between human activity and the environment.

The Seminole believed that diseases were caused by evil spirits. Until the late 1900s, they usually turned to a medicine man for a cure. He was confident that he could cure the sick person through a healing ceremony combined with the use of medicinal herbs. The ceremony involved special prayers accompanied by rattles, drums, and bells. The Seminole believed that the spirits responded to these sounds. Many of the healing herbs used have since been incorporated into modern medicines. Over the past ten to fifteen years, the Seminole have increasingly turned to doctors and hospitals when they are sick.

4 · THE PRESENT AND THE FUTURE

The Florida Seminole now number about 2,500 people. They are a small tribe that can proudly claim to be the only tribe that never surrendered to the U.S. military. Most of the Seminole now live on one of five reservations. The largest is a 52,000-acre (28,000-hectare) tract at Big Cypress in the southern part of the Everglades.

During a process called retribalization, the Florida Seminole were reorganized by the U.S. government in 1957. This change let the tribe manage its own affairs and still remain eligible for government programs, such as aid to small businesses. Seminole children go to public schools and are required to stay in school until age sixteen. The tribe is governed by a five-member council, and each reservation elects one of the council members. The council also manages tribal business investments. The Seminole have been so

The Seminole are proud of their heritage and the public schools they have established.

successful that other tribes often come to them for advice.

Most families in Oklahoma and Florida now live in modern homes, although some people in the Everglades still live in chickees. Chickees are popular not only in reservation communities but throughout southern Florida as an important symbol of the traditional life of the Seminole people.

The Seminole now work at typical jobs—as store clerks, office and construction workers, and tour guides—but a few have unusual jobs such as alligator wrestling. The tribe's recent ventures into a casino and bingo hall have helped the Seminole invest in a luxury hotel and spa. Profits also provide college scholarships for young Seminole and free job training for those who are unemployed.

The future for the Florida Seminole is highly uncertain. Some young people are more interested in being part of mainstream American society than in their tribal customs, but many are intent on preserving their Seminole heritage. The future of the Everglades is also unknown. The region is of vital importance in terms of economic potential and environmental significance. The Army Corps of Engineers has spent years building canals and drainage ditches to control the flow of water from Lake Okeechobee. This has turned one-fifth of the Everglades into prime agricultural land. Environmentalists say that interference with the Everglades is destroying one of America's most valuable wetlands. But

An alligator "farm" draws tourists to the Seminole reservation.

Charlie Cypress and the Dugout Canoe

In the 1990s, the Seminole tribal council realized that their traditional dugout canoes were rapidly being replaced by modern boats. To preserve the dugout craft, the council hired a Seminole expert named Charlie Cypress to make a dugout canoe and videotape the process. The task requires great patience and skill. After burning away much of the log and scraping out the charred wood, Charlie Cypress made the traditional prow in an elegant curve, as if the canoe were going to rise out of the water. He also made the bottom flat so that the canoe could be poled through shallow waters with speed. Charlie Cypress's completed canoe is now on display at the Smithsonian Institution in Washington, D.C.

Dugout canoes provided easy transportation through the Everglades.

supporters say that the farmland is essential for supplying garden vegetables to much of the North. Some people call the Everglades farming district the "Vegetable Kingdom." The introduction of beef cattle in the 1950s added to the region's importance, and so has the creation of Everglades National Park.

Herds of beef cattle have added to the Seminole's growing prosperity.

· TIME LINE

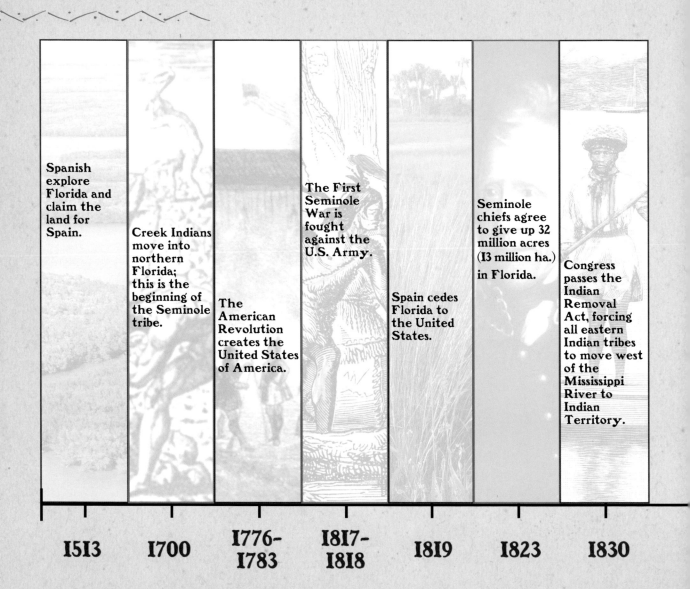

Spanish explore Florida and claim the land for Spain.

Creek Indians move into northern Florida; this is the beginning of the Seminole tribe.

The American Revolution creates the United States of America.

The First Seminole War is fought against the U.S. Army.

Spain cedes Florida to the United States.

Seminole chiefs agree to give up 32 million acres (13 million ha.) in Florida.

Congress passes the Indian Removal Act, forcing all eastern Indian tribes to move west of the Mississippi River to Indian Territory.

1513   1700   1776–1783   1817–1818   1819   1823   1830

Osceola leads the Seminole in the Second Seminole War.

The Second Seminole War ends; hundreds of Seminole are forced to move to Indian Territory.

The Third Seminole War ends when Chief Billy Bowlegs leads a small group to Indian Territory.

The Citizenship Act makes all Indians U.S. citizens.

U.S. government officially recognizes the Seminole tribe of Florida.

Indian Religious Freedom Act guarantees the right to practice traditional religions.

U.S. government recognizes the right of the tribes to open gambling casinos. These casinos now exist in twenty-nine states.

1835   1842   1855-1858   1924   1957   1978   1988

· GLOSSARY

breechcloth: Simple garment worn by men that reached from the waist to the upper thigh.

chickees: Seminole houses made of a raised platform, a roof made of leaves, and no walls.

cimarron: Spanish word for "wild."

clan: A small band of Indians, usually made up of people related by blood.

medicine bundle: A collection of bits of stone, feathers, deer-skin, and other items kept by the medicine man and believed to hold symbols of everything that the tribe needs to survive and prosper.

saw grass: The tall grasses of the Everglades that have sharp, teethlike blades along their edges.

Seminole patchwork: The unique Seminole craft made by sewing together different-colored bands of cloth to form beautiful patterns.

sofkee: A standard Seminole food made of cornmeal.

· FIND OUT MORE

Books

Brooks, Barbara. *The Seminole*. Vero Beach, FL: Rourke Publications, Inc., 1989.

Corwin, Judith Hoffman. *Native American Crafts of the Northeast and Southeast*. New York: Franklin Watts, 2002.

Murdoch, David. *North American Indians: Eyewitness Books*. New York: DK Publishing, 1992.

Ortiz, Simon. *The People Shall Continue*. Chicago: Children's Book Press, 1992.

Utley, Robert, and Wilcomb E. Washburn. *The American Heritage History of the Indian Wars*. New York: American Heritage Publishing Co., 1977.

Web Sites

www.nativeculture.com

A general listing of hundreds of resources

www.nmai.si.edu

Introduces users to the National Museum of the American Indian

About the Author

David C. King is an award-winning author who has written more than forty books for children and young adults, including *Projects About Ancient Egypt* in the Hands-On History series. He and his wife, Sharon, live in the Berkshires at the junction of New York, Massachusetts, and Connecticut.

• INDEX

Page numbers in **boldface** are illustrations.

48